OVERCOMING THE FEAR OF DEATH

&

INEVITABLE PREPARATION

10 STRATEGIES FOR OVERCOMING FEAR OF DEATH

LINDA COOPER

Published by Franklin Publishers
Printed in the United States of America

For permissions, inquiries, or additional copies, contact:
Franklin Publishers
www.franklinpublishers.com

DEDICATION

This book is dedicated to my children, grandchildren, great-grandchild, nieces, nephews, and sisters, one still on the land of the living and one of the angels who has been assigned to watch over me, L.C., along with my mother and brother.

This book is also dedicated to those who are fearing to face the death of their loved ones or themselves.

Helloooo...! "YOU ARE GONNA DIE," PERIOD POINT BLANK!!! Get used to it; we are not going to be here forever, and nothing is going to last forever, so what are you doing to prepare?

ACKNOWLEDGMENTS

I want to first and foremost thank God my Father for His goodness and mercy shown toward me. There have been so many, even in the family, who didn't believe this would ever happen. Well, thanks to all those who didn't believe this book would ever come to fruition. Naysayers were the fuel underneath my wings. Some children kept pushing me to move forward with this project. If you can dream it, if you can see it, then you can have it, is my motto. Don't ever let what others say to you or about you stop you from accomplishing your dream. Regardless of your age, keep going forward! God is with you, He said He would never leave you nor forsake you! God Bless!

Table of Contents

INTRODUCTION

*"Have not I commanded thee? Be strong and of
a good courage; be not afraid, neither be thou
dismayed: for the LORD thy God is with thee
whithersoever thou goest." - Joshua 1:9*

Is it not amazing that the Bible says "fear not" in about 365 times? You see, fear is not from God, not even the fear of death. Although God pronounced death on the entire human race because of sin, the fear of death does not come from Him.

After the death of Moses, God had to speak courage into Joshua. There were tendencies that fear had gripped his heart, but God commanded him not to be afraid. From this account, it becomes clear that strongness coupled with courage is a must, not an option.

David confessed in Psalm 23:4 that even though he passes through the valley of the shadow of death, he will not fear because the presence of God is with him. Just as God promised to be with Joshua, His presence is over and around your life. You don't have to be afraid of death of any kind. Yes, life is a preparation for death, and death is an inevitable end.

However, we must dispel the fear of death from our hearts. Anything that causes you to fear death is not from God. Death is an unavoidable part of the cycle of life, yet many of us do everything we can to avoid accepting our mortality. But coming to terms with the inevitability of death can help teach us to live more fully in the here and now.

I believe so much in the Bible, and I trust you do too. Let me share a powerful revelation from the scriptures about death in *Hebrews 2:14-15: "Since all his 'children' have flesh and blood, so Jesus became human to fully identify with us. He did this, so that he could experience death and annihilate the effects of the intimidating accuser who holds against us the power of death. By embracing death Jesus sets free those who live their entire lives in bondage to the tormenting dread of death" (TPT).*

You can read that passage again until the reality of victory over death settles in you. Jesus died so that you will not experience the tormenting dread of death. He has annihilated death's intimidating power and given us peace and freedom. Death is oppressive. On the other hand, oppression is a leading activity of demons. But we have been given authority over the spirit that causes the fear of death.

This book, *"Overcoming the Fear of Death and the Inevitable Preparation,"* will open your understanding to the truths of God's word and help you gain your freedom from the fear of death in all ways. You already have authority over fear in Christ; you only need to exercise that authority.

2 Timothy 1:7 says: "For God will never give you the spirit of fear, but the Holy Spirit who gives you mighty power, love, and self-control" (TPT). You can now believe that fear is not from God. He has given you the spirit of power, love, and a sound mind to combat the spirit of fear.

As you read this book, I am ensured you will apply the Word of God to your heart and life. Confess what the Word of God says concerning you. There also may be times in our lives when we need to prepare for the death of toxic relationships. However, you will not die until you fulfill God's purpose for your life here.

So, "What You Do Makes a Difference, And You Have to Decide What Kind of Difference You Want to Make".

-Jane Goodall

Death, be not proud, though some have called thee
Mighty and dreadful, for thou art not so;
For those whom thou think'st thou dost overthrow
Die not, poor Death, nor yet canst thou kill me.

From rest and sleep, which but thy pictures be,
Much pleasure; then from thee much more must flow,
And soonest our best men with thee do go,
Rest of their bones, and soul's delivery.

Thou art slave to Fate, Chance, kings, and desperate men,
And dost with poison, war, and sickness dwell,
And poppy or charms can make us sleep as well
And better than thy stroke; why swell'st thou then?
One short sleep past, we wake eternally,
And Death shall be no more; Death, thou shalt die.

Death, Be Not Proud

By John Donne

PART 1

EMBRACING THE CYCLE OF LIFE

"He hath made everything beautiful in his time...I know that there is no good in them, but for a man to rejoice, and to do good in his life. And also that every man should eat and drink, and enjoy the good of all his labour, it is the gift of God" - Ecclesiastes 3:11-13

Life is beautiful! and it's full of cycles; we celebrate births, we mourn over deaths, we course through the highs and lows, and we embrace new beginnings and endings. Knowing that this cycle of life will come to an end one day, should we live in constant panic? In fear? In sorrow? No! I don't think so. I really think we need to appreciate every moment we are able to breathe and make every minute of our lives worth it. Life is lived once, and there's a lot we can live for; family, purpose, legacy, the list goes on.

In the story of my life, I have begun to embrace the cycle of what life brings. Life has been good for me. I am given a wonderful family, a beautiful home with my daughter and her family, where I currently reside, and a challenging career that supports my lifestyle. I live my life in the now without worrying about what the future may bring or what my past may cause. I know that every second of my day is precious; therefore, I go about my day with gusto. Life is too short to live in fear of things that may never happen. Each day brings a new beginning, and I rise, THANKING GOD for a chance to make my life better and an opportunity to make a difference in someone else's life. I wake up each morning with a humble attitude and flash a smile to each person I encounter. I admit that the final stage of the cycle of life used to scare me, but my mother, brother, sister, and friends that I love dearly have prepared me.

I came to the conclusion that it is perfectly normal to be afraid of death because it brings uncertainty. However, I refrain from worrying about it! I am sure that it will all be okay! I embrace the cycle of life for whatever it is. I live a fruitful life and hope to have many years left to experience. **Stop fearing the cycle of life!** Today is the day. I feel thankful for what I have been given and graciously anticipate what is yet to come because this is the day my Lord has made, and I will rejoice in it! (Psalms 118:24)

Self-Reflection Questions

1. What are the 10 best experiences I have had in my life?

2. Why am I afraid of death?

3. How can I become more comfortable with the thought of aging or dying?

Now, I would like to introduce Strategies that will help you embrace life and deal with your fear of death.

Strategy #1: Reduce Your Fear of Death & Embrace the Present

Losing someone can't be easy, and grieving is different with everyone. Grieving the loss of a loved one permits you to be who you are and where you are in your journey.

Every earthly organism naturally strives to live as long as possible. If you're spending too much time worrying about the prospect of dying, you're missing out on life! When confronting fears about death and life's uncertainties, the key is learning to accept what has been and focus on what can be while you prepare for what will be.

1. Accept that every living thing dies eventually

Nothing is more natural than death. It's a necessary process to make room for new life to thrive. Consider how crowded it would be if all the animals and people from 500 years ago were still roaming around. It would be a tough thing on the social security system as well.

2. Explore your spirituality and religions

It might be argued that all religions were developed to ease the fear and discomfort of death. Take a deeper look at topics in spirituality and religion. There are so many options. You're likely to find something that resonates with your personality and beliefs, which will help you with your personal quest for meaning of life.

3. Focus on enjoying your life

Decide to get the most out of your life right now. *Shift your focus to the joys of life and fulfilling your dreams.* Be mindful. Live in the present moment. You'll find that you spend less and less time worrying about death. Why look back when your future is ahead. Concentrate on keeping joy in your heart, because the scripture says, *"Do not grieve, for the joy of the Lord is our Strength" (Nehemiah 8:10)*

4. Read a book

Fear of death is common. The subject has been covered extensively by experts. A few suggestions are: "Grieving the Loss of a Loved One" by Kathe Wunnenberg. There are plenty of books and support groups focused on the subject of death. Read a chapter each week and put the ideas into action. Avoid rushing through. Information that isn't used is wasted. Take your time and contemplate the author's message.

5. Be grateful for what you have

Focusing on death is focusing on loss. Yes, you've lost a loved one that is close to your heart, but how do you get through this? Choose to focus on the wonderful things and people you already have in your life. Find ways to feel good and try to stay in that mental space. *Feeling good is a habit that you can develop.*

6. Make plans for the future that excite you

Give yourself something positive to look forward to. Instead of worrying or distracting yourself in an unhealthy manner, make plans or set goals that inspire you. Begin today by creating a huge list of everything you want to see and do.

7. Try a new activity

Jump into something you've never done before. Take a painting class or join a bowling team. A little novelty can show you that there are still plenty of interesting things left to experience. *Give yourself a reason to be excited about life.* Stepping into anything new, no matter how small can help you understand that you are capable of more than you think. The mindset you build is just as important as the activity itself. You begin to accept the thought that joy and fulfillment lie in the unknown. It serves as a reminder that even when life appears to be predictable, there are still opportunities for thrill and amazement. Allow yourself to experiment, and do not be afraid to fail along the road. Every new experience, whether successful or not, teaches you something and leaves you with memories that enrich your life.

You'll also learn more about yourself—your likes, dislikes, strengths, and possibly even hidden abilities. So go ahead and try something new. It may become your next passion or at the very least, a reason to smile and enjoy life a little more.

8. Spend more time with your friends and loved ones

Spending more time with friends and family is one of the most effective antidotes to anxiety and fear. When you're feeling overwhelmed, being with people who care about you can give you a sense of relief, stability, and perspective. Friends and family may provide emotional support while also reminding you of who you truly are—someone cherished and valued. Simply sitting in the presence of someone you trust, without saying anything, can be enough to relax your thoughts and bring you serenity.

Sharing your problems openly with individuals close to you relieves the emotional burden. You don't have to carry everything alone, and talking about your anxieties can help you gain a new perspective. Even if your loved ones are unable to remedy the problem for you, simply having someone listen and validate your feelings makes a significant difference. They may also give insight or advise based on their own experiences to help you handle challenging emotions.

Spending time with older individuals can be especially illuminating. They frequently have a wealth of personal experience and insight to impart. They've most certainly endured their own concerns and problems, and their perspective might serve as a reminder that difficulties are just temporary and that life has a way of working itself out. Connecting with others who know and care for you, whether through a meal, a walk, or simply chatting, provides a grounding experience that helps you put things in perspective. In their company, fear begins to lose its hold.

9. Prepare

Your anxiety can be rooted in the impact your passing would have on your loved ones left behind. Get your affairs in order and eliminate the cause of your worry to the best of your ability. What's priceless is your" Peace Of Mind" because you have planned ahead by acquiring a final expense insurance or a pre-burial policy to ease the burden of preparing for the inevitable. It's natural to think about your mortality. However, spending too much time worrying about the inevitable is time poorly spent. Examine the cause of your fear and find ways to address it. Everyone is dying. *Everyone is also living.* Seize your time here and make the most of it. When you're focused on life, your fear of death tends to dissipate.

Embracing the circle of life teaches us to love the present, let go of the past, and face the eventual fact of death with fortitude. Living completely entails not becoming stuck by yesterday's regrets or tomorrow's concerns but rather embracing the beauty of the present. When we embrace life, we prepare for the future with purpose rather than despair. Confronting our fear of mortality allows us to live more freely, knowing that every moment counts and that every decision we make can build a legacy that will outlive us. When we live intentionally, we walk in confidence, trusting that the future is in God's hands. This will allow us to let go of fear and truly live.

Sunset and evening star,
And one clear call for me!
And may there be no moaning of the bar,
When I put out to sea,
But such a tide as moving seems asleep,
Too full for sound and foam,
When that which drew from out the boundless deep
Turns again home.

Twilight and evening bell,
And after that the dark!
And may there be no sadness of farewell,
When I embark;

For though from out our bourne of Time and Place
The flood may bear me far,
I hope to see my Pilot face to face
When I have crossed the bar.

Crossing the Bar

By Alfred Lord Tennyson

PART 2

SURVIVING THE UNTIMELY DEATH OF A LOVED ONE

---

*"Be of good courage, and he shall strengthen
your heart, all ye that hope in the Lord"
- Psalm 31:24*

Have you lost someone you love dearly? Many times, these deaths come as the result of long illnesses, but sometimes, the deaths are sudden and unexpected. In either case, grief can be overwhelming. Losing someone we love is one of the hardest things we can experience in this life. When that loss is unexpected or untimely, it can shake us to our core. Grief can be overpowering, whether due to the suddenness of it all or the sense that things were left unsaid. In times like these, several questions can rush through our minds with no one to answer: Why did this happen? How do I move forward? Will the pain ever end?

First, let me say this, you're not the first to lose someone dear to you. We've all walked through the valley of grief at some point, and the Bible acknowledges the depth of that pain. *Psalm 34:18 says, "The Lord is close to the brokenhearted and saves those who are crushed in spirit."* God sees you in your grief, and He's near, even when it doesn't feel like it. The death of a loved one might make you feel as though a part of yourself has been taken away. During a period of grief, one's normal day-to-day activities need a significantly higher level of energy. Dealing with the pain effectively can help you pick up the pieces that are left and continue to live. While there is no quick fix to surviving the loss of a loved one, there are steps we can take to heal and find hope again.

Self-Reflection Questions

1. Am I allowing myself to truly grieve?

2. Do I blame myself or others for the loss?

3. How can I keep their memory alive while moving forward?

Strategy #2: Overcome Grief & Move Forward

1. Acknowledge the Pain—Grief Is Not a Straight Line

There is no timeline for grief, and there's no "right way" to grieve. One day, you might feel okay, and the next day, the sadness might hit like a wave. Allow yourself to ride those waves without judgment. *Psalm 30:5 offers us hope when we are in deep pain: "Weeping may stay for the night, but rejoicing comes in the morning."* Remember, there's no rush to get through it.

2. Take Your Grief to God in Prayer

There are moments when words fail us when the pain is too deep for us to even express. Romans 8:26 tells us, "The Spirit helps us in our weakness. We do not know what we ought to pray for, but the Spirit himself intercedes for us through wordless groans." When you don't know what to pray, trust that God understands. Bring your broken heart to Him and let Him hold you in those moments.

3. Surround yourself with support

At first, you could feel the need to be left alone with your thoughts, or you might be intimidated by the prospect of loving another person again. The feelings that you are experiencing are perfectly natural and even expected. Isolating oneself, on the other hand, may prove to be counterproductive to your effort to get better. Isolation can make grief worse. Reach out to those who love you, whether that's family, friends, or even a support group. Sometimes, you just need to talk about your loved one, and that's okay. Proverbs 17:17 says, "A friend loves at all times, and a brother is born for a time of adversity." Lean on the people who care about you—they want to be there for you.

Accept the support of others. It is true that people may occasionally say the incorrect thing, but the vast majority of them have a genuine desire to assist. Try to find someone to talk to and be honest about how you are feeling. You should take advantage of the fact that people are willing to bring you a meal or spend the evening with you. Everyone needs support through difficult times.

4. Keep it real

Recognize and embrace your emotions, and be truthful with yourself about how you are feeling. When you are grieving, there is no correct or incorrect way to convey your emotions. Part of the healing process involves allowing your emotions, however intense, to come out freely. Sometimes, after losing someone, we feel guilty for experiencing moments of joy—like we're betraying their memory by smiling again. But remember, joy and sorrow can coexist.

5. Express yourself

Feel free to talk about your loss with your support network. If you're not ready to communicate your feelings face to face, write a blog or join an online community of others with similar experiences.

6. Take care of yourself

Stay as true to your everyday routine as you can. Regular exercise and healthy nutrition contribute to your overall emotional wellness. Go above and above your typical loving routine and treat yourself to a relaxing massage, a walk in nature, or some time to listen to soothing music. *Nehemiah 8:10 says, "The joy of the Lord is your strength."* You can laugh again, enjoy life again, and still honor your loved one. They wouldn't want you to live in sorrow forever.

7. Educate yourself

Make research on the topic of grief in order to learn the signs and strategies for coping with it. Educating yourself on the subject can be essential to the healing process. As you do your research, you'll begin to understand your feelings. You'll discover that others who have lost someone they love also feel your feelings, and you'll learn about what others have done to work through grief.

8. Create a Meaningful Memorial for Your Loved One

Doing something tangible to remember your loved one can bring comfort. Whether it's planting a tree in their honor, setting aside a special day each year to celebrate their life, or creating a memory book, you should find a way to keep their memory alive. This can help you process your grief while also celebrating the impact they had on your life.

9. Take it one day at a time

When you're faced with death, all you may see is a blank wall in front of you. Looking beyond the tragedy and thinking about life without your loved one may feel exceedingly tough. Your feelings may be so strong that they blur your perception.

Certainly, life will never be the same, and you must learn to adjust to living with the absence. However, there's a brighter picture hidden beyond that wall, which you'll soon be able to see it.

10. Seek Professional Counseling if Needed

Sometimes, the weight of grief can be too heavy to carry alone. There's no shame in seeking professional help from a counseling psychologist or therapist. Proverbs 15:22 says, "Plans fail for lack of counsel, but with many advisers they succeed." Talking to someone who understands the process of grief can help you through those difficult times.

Moving forward following the untimely death of a loved one does not imply forgetting them. In reality, you may honor their memory by living fully and discovering ways to celebrate their life that offer you peace, such as creating a meaningful custom or doing something that reflects who they were. *Ecclesiastes 3:1 says, "There is a time for everything and a season for every activity under the heavens."* While mourning is a necessary part of the journey, there will come a time when you may embrace life again, bringing their legacy with you.

Grieving takes time, so be kind to yourself. Set minor goals, celebrate successes, and be aware that special occasions such as birthdays or holidays may bring new pain. However, these moments can also be used to honor a loved one. And if you discover joy again by having fun, you may ask yourself, "How dare I enjoy life without my loved one present?" But in reality, you're not betraying your loved one by having fun, don't feel bad—enjoying life isn't a betrayal. In fact, the best way to remember people we have lost is to live our lives to the fullest.

I am standing upon the seashore.
A ship at my side spreads her white sails to the morning
breeze and starts for the blue ocean.
She is an object of beauty and strength.

I stand and watch her until at length she hangs like a speck of white cloud
just where the sea and sky come to mingle with each other.

Then someone at my side says, "There, she is gone!"
"Gone where?"
Gone from my sight. That is all.

She is just as large in mast and hull and spar as she was when
she left my side and she is just as able to bear her load
of living freight to her destined port.
Her diminished size is in me, not in her.
And just at the moment when someone at my side says,

"There, she is gone!"
There are other eyes watching her coming, and other voices
ready to take up the glad shout,
"Here she comes!"
And that is dying.

I Am Standing Upon the Seashore

By Henry Van Dyke

PART 3

DEALING WITH THE EMOTIONAL TRAUMA OF FEELING A DECEASED LOVED ONE'S PRESENCE

"The Lord is close to the brokenhearted and
saves those who are crushed in spirit."
– Psalms 34:18

Do you sometimes feel like you are not alone despite a loved one being deceased? When someone close to us, be it a family member or a friend, passes away, it's always something painful to go through. Especially when we deeply care about our loved ones, and the pain that comes after all of the funeral ceremonies is often tough to endure. It is, regrettably, part of the cycle of life, and we can only attempt to go on and retain them in our mind.

When someone we love passes away, it can feel like a part of us is gone, too. Yet, there are moments when their presence feels so real, even though they're no longer physically with us. It is sometimes the case that the spirit of our loved ones comes to visit us and leaves us with signs that they are around. There are countless types of signs that people talk about having experienced, and some sound more credible than others.

From being able to catch their unique smell and feeling someone coming inside the room to the more tangible signs, we have gathered the most common ways to tell that a deceased loved one came to visit you!

Many people express feeling as if they have been visited by a deceased loved one, and this is not unusual. Whether you believe it's a spiritual connection, an illusion of your mind, or your brain processing grief, the emotions that come with it are so real. It's important to acknowledge how these moments affect us. They can bring peace, but they can also bring up feelings of unresolved trauma. Loss is painful, and sometimes, it leaves scars that take time to heal. But in times like these, it's helpful to think about what the Bible says about comfort and peace. According to *2 Corinthians 1:3-4, "the God of all comfort… comforts us in all our troubles, so that we can comfort those in any trouble with the comfort we ourselves receive from God."* God's comfort is with us, even during our darkest pain and moments of uncertainty.

Self-Reflection Questions

1. Have you ever felt that a deceased loved one came to visit you?

2. How do you feel when these moments happen?

3. Have these experiences helped or hindered your healing?

As I said, sometimes, these feelings of connection can bring a sense of closure or peace. Other times, they can reopen wounds. Be honest with yourself about how these experiences impact your healing. Are they helping you move forward, or do they keep you stuck in the past? Reflecting on this can guide you toward greater emotional freedom.

Strategy #3: Processing Emotions & Healing

1. Acknowledge Your Emotions

Grief can bring a whirlwind of emotions. You might feel anger, sadness, guilt, or even feel relief. Whatever you feel, it's important to acknowledge it without judgment. *"Blessed are those who mourn, for they will be comforted" (Matthew 5:4).* Jesus Himself promises comfort to those who mourn, which means you don't have to hide your feelings or pretend to be "okay" when you're not.

2. Pray and Seek God's Comfort

When you feel overwhelmed by the emotions of grief or the unsettling feeling of a loved one's presence, take it to God in prayer. *Psalm 34:18 says, "The Lord is close to the brokenhearted and saves those who are crushed in spirit."* God is always near, ready to provide peace and strength when we need it most. Ask Him to guide you through these feelings and help you heal.

3. Talk About Your Feelings with Someone You Trust

Sometimes, the best way to process grief is by talking it out with someone. Whether it's a close friend, a pastor, or a counselor, sharing your experiences can lighten the emotional load. Proverbs 11:14 reminds us that "Where there is no counsel, the people fall; but in the multitude of counselors, there is safety." There's strength in seeking wise counsel and allowing others to support you through your grief journey.

4. Understand the Impact of Trauma

Grief, especially after a traumatic loss, can leave deep emotional scars. These scars can resurface when you least expect them—like during those moments when you feel your loved one's presence. Trauma isn't just about what happened at the time of loss but how the mind and body continue to process it. Understanding this can help you take steps toward healing. *Psalm 147:3 tells us that "He heals the brokenhearted and binds up their wounds."* Healing is a process, and God is at work in your heart, even when you don't see it right away.

5. Create Space for Healing Rituals

For many, finding a way to honor a loved one helps in processing grief. This could be through lighting a candle, visiting a favorite place of theirs, or simply setting aside quiet time to reflect and pray. These small acts can provide a sense of closure and peace, allowing you to remember them without the weight of unresolved emotions. *"Come to me, all you who are weary and burdened, and I will give you rest" (Matthew 11:28).* Jesus invites us to find rest in Him, even as we carry the burdens of grief and trauma.

6. Embrace the Peace That Comes from Letting Go

It's natural to hold onto the memory of a loved one, but sometimes we unknowingly hold onto the pain, too. There's a difference between remembering with love and clinging to unresolved grief. Letting go doesn't mean forgetting—it means releasing the pain so you can live fully in the present. Philippians 4:7 speaks of "the peace of God, which transcends all understanding, [that] will guard your hearts and your minds in Christ Jesus." Trust that God's peace will fill the spaces where fear and sorrow once resided.

Grief is a unique experience for each individual. You may feel closer to a loved one after they have died, and you may also feel overwhelmed by the loss. Not only is God with you every step of this experience, but he also has provided you with people, resources, and His Word to rely on for support. Let go of your fear and allow the healing that comes from time, prayer, and guidance. "The Lord is my light and my salvation—whom shall I fear?" (Psalms 27:1). I pray you find comfort, strength, and peace beyond comprehension during these times.

Sleep on, beloved, sleep, and take thy rest;
Lay down thy head upon the Savior's breast;
We love thee well, but Jesus loves thee best—
Good-night! Good-night! Good-night!

Calm is thy slumber as an infant's sleep;
But thou shalt wake no more to toil and weep;
Thine is a perfect rest, secure and deep—
Good-night! Good-night! Good-night!

Until the shadows from this earth are cast,
Until He gathers in His sheaves at last,
Until the twilight gloom is overpast—
Good-night! Good-night! Good-night!

The Christian's Good-night

By Sarah Doudney

PART 4

BECOMING FEARLESS

"Yea, though I walk through the valley of the shadow of death, I will fear no evil: for thou art with me; thy rod and thy staff they comfort me"
- Psalm 23:4

You sometimes get afraid, don't you? Fear is something we all face, whether we like to admit it or not. It's human. But have you ever stopped to think about how much of your life is shaped by fear? What if you could let go of those fears? Imagine how different things could be if you lived without that constant shadow hanging over you. That's what we're diving into now—what it means to become fearless, especially when it comes to the biggest fear of all: death.

One of the most powerful verses about fear is found in *2 Timothy 1:7: "For God has not given us a spirit of fear, but of power and of love and of a sound mind."* This verse reminds us that fear doesn't come from God. Instead, He gives us the strength and clarity we need to face our fears and overcome them.

Self-Reflection Questions

1. What do my greatest fears reveal about me?
2. How can I overcome habits that reinforce my fears?
3. How would being fearless change my life?

Strategy #4: Teach Yourself to Become Fearless

1. Trust in God's Presence and Promises

The first step to becoming fearless is to remember that God is always with us right there where we are. He's no longer interested in what had been or what could have been but your present state. God is present in that situation to help you overcome it; you only have to be courageous. Remember God's message to Joshua right after the demise of Moses in chapter 1, verse 9 of the book of Joshua: "Be strong and courageous. Do not be afraid; do not be discouraged, for the Lord your God will be with you wherever you go." When we know that God is by our side, there's nothing we need to fear. Whether it's fear of the unknown or fear of failure, His promises are our safety net.

2. Live in the Moment

This key has really worked for me. I always choose to live in the moment and avoid anticipating everything that could go wrong.

Although, it is wise to make plans for typical challenges, like traffic delays and bad weather. But it is also essential to realize that many events are beyond our control. So, living each moment fully not only allows us to enjoy the present but also prepares us to be fearless. When we focus on the present moment rather than thinking about what might go wrong, we break free from fear. Understanding that we don't have control over everything and choosing to trust God is a great way to live fearlessly.

By living in the present, we remind ourselves that fear does not have to control our behaviors or emotions. Instead of allowing fear about the future to consume us, we rely on God's strength and power to face each day with confidence. The more we let go of fear and trust in God's plan, the more fearless we will be in pursuing our purpose and enjoying a joyful and peaceful life.

3. Challenge Negative Thoughts

Fear often comes from the negative stories we tell ourselves. "I can't do this." "What if I fail?" "I'm not good enough." These thoughts only feed our fears. Instead, challenge them with God's truth. When those fearful thoughts creep in, remind yourself of verses like *Romans 8:37: "In all these things we are more than conquerors through Him who loved us."* Replace lies with truth, and fear will start to fade. Greater understanding makes life less scary. I do teach myself to let go of whatever is causing my distress. When I am terrified, I bring my anxieties out into the open. Focusing on my breathing dispels my anxieties. My muscles relax, and my thoughts become purified. You, too, can try that.

4. Surround Yourself with Encouraging People

Fear can grow when we feel isolated or unsupported. Proverbs 27:17 says, "As iron sharpens iron, so one person sharpens another." Surrounding yourself with people who encourage and uplift you is key to building courage. These are the people who will remind you of your strengths and God's promises when fear tries to pull you down. Don't be afraid to lean on such people in difficult times.

5. Trust Yourself to Face it!

I face hardships head-on. I trust myself to manage whatever comes my way. Looking back on past adversities shows me that I can win over challenging situations. I may get a better job once I get laid off from one work. I may learn to manage a chronic medical condition by simple changes to my lifestyle. Taking prompt action teaches me that I am resilient. Finding solutions becomes my focus. I acknowledge my feelings. I take it easy with myself when I feel anxious. At the same time, I decide to continue ahead anyhow, and anxiety shifts to the background. As the popular saying goes, "Do the thing you fear, and the death of fear is certain." The more you face your fears, the weaker your fears become.

6. Lean on God's Strength, Not Your Own

Sometimes, we try to overcome fear on our own, but I have never tried that. I know it will never work out it'll only lead to feeling overwhelmed. The truth is, we don't have to do it alone. God is our strength, and when we lean on Him, we find the courage we need. *Psalm 46:1 reads, "God is our refuge and strength, an ever-present help in trouble."* When fear threatens to consume you, turn to God. He will give you the strength to stand tall and face whatever comes your way.

7. Keep Your Eyes on the Bigger Picture

Fear often magnifies the immediate situation and makes us forget the bigger picture. But when we keep our eyes on God's greater plan for our lives, fear begins to shrink. *As Romans 8:28 says, "And we know that in all things God works for the good of those who love him, who have been called according to his purpose."* Trust that even when things seem uncertain, God is working things out for your good. Fear doesn't stand a chance when we're confident in God's purpose.

Becoming fearless is something that develops over time; it requires faith, trust, and a willingness to face what scares us. But with God on our side, there's no fear we can't overcome. Being courageous doesn't mean fear is not present; it means choosing to act in faith despite the fear.

"The Lord is my light and my salvation—whom shall I fear? The Lord is the stronghold of my life—of whom shall I be afraid?" Psalm 27:1 (NIV). With God as your stronghold, you can face anything fearlessly.

In my experiences, I have learned that being fearless liberates us from the restrictions we place upon ourselves. When I decided to face my fears, opportunities expanded, my mind became peaceful, and I accomplished more. Rather than wanting shelter from difficulties, I wanted the capacity to rise to any challenge. What helped my boldness when facing my fears? I acknowledged that I create my own fears. That means I also have the power to extinguish them with God's help. Today, I show great courage. I face my fears boldly and watch them go away.

No coward soul is mine,
No trembler in the world's storm-troubled sphere:
I see Heaven's glories shine,
And faith shines equal, arming me from fear.

O God within my breast,
Almighty, ever-present Deity!
Life—that in me has rest,
As I—undying Life—have power in Thee!

No Coward Soul is Mine

By Emily Brontë

PART 5

OVERCOMING THE FEAR
OF THE UNKNOWN

"And we know that all things work together for good to them that love God, to them who are the called according to his purpose" - Romans 8:28

The truth is, whether subtle or great, we all have a fear of what is not known to us. Whether it's the future, an unexpected life change, or even the question of what happens after death, the unknown has a way of making us feel vulnerable and unsettled.

It is not possible to eliminate the uncertainty; instead, we must change how we respond to it. While certain things remain unknown to us, I am personally comforted knowing that God knows it all and my life and my future is safe in his hands: "For I know the plans I have for you," says the Lord, "plans to prosper you and not to harm you; plans to give you hope and a future" (Jeremiah 29:11). This assurance allows me to let go of fear and believe that God is guiding me, even when I don't see the whole picture.

Overcoming the fear of the unknown can be a very challenging process, but it is possible. If you suffer from a fear of uncertainty, understanding what fear is and how it affects you can start you on the road to conquering it.

Fear has been defined in numerous ways; nevertheless, the most basic definition of fear is an emotional response based on the fact that we're faced with something new or impending danger. When we experience terror, multiple psychological and physiological processes take residence in our minds all at the same time.

Psychological events include feeling emotionally overwhelmed, having high levels of anxiety, and even feeling terrified. Physiological responses include a quicker heart rate, shallow breathing, and similar consequences.

Experiencing fear can tremendously affect your vision on life, your confidence levels, and even the potential that you have as a person.

Here's an example of a situation where a woman had the crippling fear that everything she did would fail:

Janice was incredibly successful in her profession and personal life. It seemed like people were quickly drawn to her and her ideas, but within her, Janice was a total mess.

Every time she takes up a project, she would pour herself into it. In the end, she would ultimately succeed, but on the inside, she was always worried that she would fail or that her completed project wouldn't be good enough.

For the most part, she recognized the fact that her fear was irrational. But Janice was raised up in an abusive environment. She was physically beaten and consistently ridiculed by her father. Regardless of what she did, it was never enough to meet his expectations.

The end result was that she grew up to become a workaholic, often striving to do numerous things at once and leaving very little time for herself.

The foundation of her fear of failing was grounded in her youth. Her father carried overly high expectations and would be mentally and physically aggressive towards her when his standards weren't satisfied. Once she learned this about her experience, Janice was able to lighten her expectations and overcome her fear.

Self-Reflection Questions

1. What is it about the unknown that scares me the most?

2. How have I dealt with unknowns in the past?

Strategy #5: Acknowledge the Reality of Uncertainties & Deal with It!

1. Accept That Uncertainty Is Part of Life

The first step is to recognize that uncertainty is a natural aspect of life. No matter how hard we attempt to prepare or predict, there will always be things beyond our control. And that's fine. "The only constant thing in life is change," as the proverb goes. The more we accept that life is full of surprises and twists, the less the influence of the unknown will hold over us. *"Do not be anxious about anything, but in every situation, by prayer and petition, with thanksgiving, present your requests to God"* *(Philippians verses 4–6).*

2. Recognize your fears

By realizing that you're fearful, you're more likely to get to the bottom of what the fear is.

- You may also have a fear of facing your fears. The best way to conquer this fear is to accept the truth behind what's causing you to experience limited happiness in life.

- You might come to understand that you're afraid of failing or taking chances. You may also feel scared because you simply don't have confidence in yourself.

- Regardless of the issue at hand, it's important that you recognize your fear and attempt to define what it is that makes you terrified of the unknown. The key here is not to dwell on your fear but rather to understand precisely what it is you're worried and afraid of.

3. Determine the underlying root of your fears.

How can you pinpoint the cause of your fears? A clever look at your life can give the answer. By recognizing what causes your fears, you can likely overcome them with great success!

4. Focus on What You Can Control

In situations like this, it is common for us to feel powerless over the situation and start feeling anxious to the point of making hasty decisions. But there are always aspects of life that we can control—our actions, our responses, and our attitude. Focus on what you can do in the present moment rather than getting lost in your thoughts. Ask yourself: "What are the steps that I can take today that will help me feel a bit more grounded even if the outcome is unclear?" There's a wisdom in Matthew 6:33, which says, *"But seek first the Kingdom of God and His righteousness, and all these things will be added unto you."* I view this scripture from a different perspective as I write this, although it's about the kingdom of God, it also offers us wisdom that **when we focus on the right things, everything else will fall into place**.

5. Face your fears

Once you've recognized your fear and understood the main cause, you're ready to tackle it! The greatest technique to achieve this is to face it head-on. Decide to purposely tackle your fears by indulging yourself in activities that push you outside of your comfort zone. For example, put yourself in a place where you're safe yet uncomfortable or respectfully confront someone from your past. In the end, you'll realize that you can successfully overcome your anxieties one by one!

My fear as a child was swimming. As I watched television when I was young, I'd see people swimming, and in my mind, I thought if they happened to go too far down in the water and it overpowered them, they couldn't get back up, so they drowned. This went with me all my life, so when my family or friends and I went to the beach or pool, I would stay close to the end where the water was shallow, and I could catch hold of something that would help me get out of the water. Recently, in my older years, and I mean older, I decided I wanted to conquer that fear, and that is what I'm doing even as I write this book. So, you're never too old, just keep trying and have the desire to overcome whatever fear, and God will allow you to push right through it."

Overcoming your fear of the unknown is a difficult undertaking. However, if you take the time to engage in these five steps, you'll discover renewed peace and happiness within your heart! As you work to unlock the chains that bind you to your fears, you'll enjoy a freedom that you've never felt before.

Abide with me; fast falls the eventide;
The darkness deepens; Lord, with me abide.
When other helpers fail and comforts flee,
Help of the helpless, O abide with me.

Hold Thou Thy cross before my closing eyes;
Shine through the gloom, and point me to the skies.
Heaven's morning breaks, and earth's vain shadows flee;
In life, in death, O Lord, abide with me.

Abide with Me

By Henry Francis Lyte

PART 6

I VALUE WISE COUNSELING

"Hear counsel, and receive instruction, that thou mayest be wise in thy latter end"
- Proverbs 19:20

We've all been in circumstances where we required guidance, whether it was over a major life decision or simply handling day-to-day issues. Seeking guidance is one of the most effective things we can do when we are not too sure or overwhelmed. But asking for guidance is not always simple. Pride can get in the way, and we don't want to appear weak or incompetent. Yet the Bible often reminds us that seeking wise counsel is a sign of intelligence, not weakness.

Proverbs 11:14 states: "Where there is no guidance, a people fall, but in an abundance of counselors there is safety." This verse underlines the need to surround ourselves with those who can provide wisdom and insight.

Wise words in times of confusion enable me to stay grounded like the anchor on a ship. Instead of being swayed by every wind that comes my way, I seek the advice of experienced people who genuinely care about me. Seeking wisdom keeps me from wandering in the vast ocean of opportunities. I listen to my trusted advisers and consider their advice. I use their ideas as a springboard for forming my own conclusions.

Heeding the words of the wise helps me avoid unnecessary pitfalls. Life is too short to learn every lesson through personal experience, so I save myself time and heartache by learning from the experiences of other people. Seeking counsel allows me to approach life's changes without fear, whether the issue is personal or career-related. Listening to the ideas of others helps me to see things from a different perspective, and I gain valuable insight from their observations.

When I'm deeply involved in a situation, and my emotions are running high, thinking objectively can be a challenge. That's why I turn to trusted people for wise counsel. Hearing their points of view allows me to evaluate the options I might have missed, providing clarity of mind. While it's my responsibility to seek out advice, I understand that the final decision rests with me. I must ultimately choose the path I will take

Today, I choose to seek out wise counsel. I appreciate those who love me enough to tell me things I need to hear, even if I would rather not hear them.

Self-Reflection Questions

1. When was the last time I sought advice?

2. Who can I turn to for wise counsel?

3. Why is it important to evaluate various points of view before making a final decision?

Strategy #6: Seek for Wise Counseling

1. Be Humble Enough to Ask for Help

It takes humility to admit that we don't have all the answers, but that's where growth begins. *Proverbs 12:15 tells us, "The way of fools seems right to them, but the wise listen to advice."* A willingness to seek counsel is a sign of strength, not weakness. Don't allow pride to stop you from getting the help that you need.

2. Pray for Wisdom and Discernment

Before seeking advice from others, seek God first. James 1:5 reminds us that God gives wisdom generously to those who ask. Pray for discernment, both in choosing the right counselors and in evaluating the advice you receive. God's wisdom is the foundation that will guide you through any situation in life.

3. Choose Advisors with Godly Character

Not everyone's advice will lead you in the right direction. *Proverbs 13:20 says, "Walk with the wise and become wise, for a companion of fools suffers harm."* Seek out people who live out their faith, who are rooted in God's Word, and who have a track record of making wise decisions. They are the voices worth listening to.

4. Weigh Different Perspectives Before Making a Decision

It's easy to latch onto the first piece of advice we get, especially if it aligns with what we are already thinking. But true wisdom often comes from considering multiple points of view. *Proverbs 18:17 reminds us, "In a lawsuit the first to speak seems right until someone comes forward and cross-examines."* Don't rush into decisions. Weigh the different perspectives carefully and prayerfully. There is importance in considering all sides of a story before forming an opinion.

5. Be Open to Correction, Not Just Confirmation

Sometimes, wise counsel comes in the form of correction. It is easy to seek advice from people who will tell us what we want to hear, but real growth comes when we're willing to listen to hard truths. *Proverbs 27:6 says, "Wounds from a friend can be trusted, but an enemy multiplies kisses."* A true friend will tell you what you need to hear, not just what makes you feel good.

6. Reflect on the Counsel You Receive and Seek God's Peace

After receiving advice, take time to reflect on it and pray for God's peace. Colossians 3:15 reminds us, "Let the peace of Christ rule in your hearts." If the counsel you receive leads you to peace, it's likely in alignment with God's will. But if you feel unsettled or confused, take more time to pray and seek clarity.

7. Don't Be Afraid to Reevaluate and Seek New Counsel

Sometimes, the advice you receive may need to be reevaluated as situations change. Be open to seeking new counsel when necessary. As the saying goes, "A wise man learns more from his enemies than a fool from his friends." Wisdom is a lifelong journey, and it's okay to continually seek out new perspectives as you grow.

Seeking wise counsel is an essential part of living a devoted and fearless life. Whether you're thinking about future decisions, dealing with conflict, or grieving, the appropriate guidance can make all the difference for you. *Proverbs 3:5-6 offers this advice: "Trust in the Lord with all your heart and lean not on your own understanding; in all your ways submit to Him, and He will make your paths straight."* When we seek God's wisdom and the counsel of those He has put in our lives, we can move confidently, knowing that we are receiving the greatest advice possible.

I go among the trees and sit still.
All my thoughts fly away.
I rise in the dry leaves, and the words of the tree speak to me:
Rest, rest, come and rest here.

I come into the peace of wild things
who do not tax their lives with forethought
of grief. I come into the presence of still water.
And I feel above me the day-blind stars waiting with their light.
For a little while, I rest in the grace of the world,
and I am free.

The Peace of Wild Things

By Wendell Berry

PART 7

I CONQUER MY FEARS BY RELYING ON THE CREATOR

"When I am afraid, I will trust in you, O God. In God, whose word I praise, in God I trust; I will not be afraid. What can mere mortals do to me?" - Psalm 56:3-4

"Fear is a liar." We've all heard it before, and it's true: fear is a part of life. We've all experienced it in some way, whether it's fear of the unknown, failure, or the deeper fear of death. But what if, instead of allowing fear to control us, we turned it over to the one who created us? When we put our trust in the Creator, we gain strength and peace far beyond what we could muster on our own. It is not about-facing fear alone anymore; it's about allowing God to take the lead and fight those battles on our behalf. The Bible also gives us insight that our battles are God's own to fight. (1 Samuel 17:47, 2 Chronicles 20:15).

In Isaiah 41:10, God gives us this comforting promise: "Fear not, for I am with you; be not dismayed, for I am your God. I will strengthen you and help you; I will uphold you with my righteous right hand." That's it right there. We're not expected to handle fear on our own. God is with us, ready to lift us up and give us the courage we need. So, how do we live this out?

Knowing God's promises, I take each day as it comes, I'm well informed that I have the support of a loving God to guide me through any situation I face. Whether I am afraid of the unknown, worrying about my circumstances, or doubting my own abilities, I find comfort and strength in divine guidance. Though some situations may cause fear due to their unpredictability, I lean on the Creator for the courage to face my fears head-on.

When I am about to embark on something new, I admit I get butterflies. I want to do a good job, but sometimes I doubt my own abilities. In those moments, I ask the Creator to provide the bravery I need to approach it with confidence. When my heart is racing with anxiety or fear, I rely on the Creator to calm my nerves and bring me peace, knowing I am always in capable hands.

Today, I am convinced that I am guided and protected. I remind myself that there is nothing to fear. I shatter the negative feelings that come with scary situations by calling on divine help in times of trouble.

Self-Reflection Questions

1. Do I sometimes let fear get the better of me?

2. What do I teach my children to help lessen their fears?

3. How do I react when I am surprised by an unwanted challenge?

Life undoubtedly throws challenges our way. It can be unpredictable, and things don't always go as planned. When faced with unforeseen problems, our faith is tested. *James 1:2-3 states: "Consider it pure joy, my brothers and sisters, whenever you face trials of many kinds because you know that the testing of your faith produces perseverance."* Instead of letting obstacles overwhelm you, see them as chances to strengthen your faith in God.

Strategy #7: Rest on God & His Promises

1. Let God Be Bigger Than Your Fear

Sometimes, we give our fears too much power. We focus on them until they seem insurmountable. But the truth is, God is bigger than any fear you have. *Psalm 27:1 says, "The Lord is my light and my salvation—whom shall, I fear? The Lord is the stronghold of my life—of whom shall I be afraid?"* Instead of magnifying your fears, magnify God. Remind yourself daily that He is bigger, stronger, and more capable than anything you're afraid of.

2. Surrender Control and Trust God's Plan

Fear often comes from wanting to have control over our future, our circumstances, and our lives. But here's the thing: real peace comes when we surrender that control to God. *Jeremiah 29:11 reminds us, "For I know the plans I have for you, declares the Lord, plans to prosper you and not to harm you, plans to give you hope and a future."* When you let go and trust that God's plan is better than anything you could orchestrate, fear loses its grip.

3. Feed Your Faith, Not Your Fear

With these words "fear" and "faith" which should come first alphabetically? Faith, of course, because "fa" comes before "fe" in Fear. God is already pointing us to what to seek first. What we focus on grows. If you focus on your fears, they'll seem bigger and more overwhelming. But if you focus on your faith in God's promises, your fears will shrink. *Romans 10:17 says, "So faith comes from hearing, and hearing through the word of Christ."* Spend time in Scripture, listen to uplifting sermons, and surround yourself with people who remind you of God's faithfulness. When your faith is strong, your fears won't stand a chance.

4. Lean Into Prayer During Moments of Anxiety

When fear strikes, turn to prayer. Philippians 4:6-7 encourages us, "Do not be anxious about anything, but in every situation, by prayer and petition, with thanksgiving, present your requests to God. And the peace of God, which transcends all understanding, will guard your hearts and your minds in Christ Jesus." Prayer is your direct line to the Creator, who loves you and cares about every detail of your life. When anxiety hits, pause, pray, and let His peace wash over you. Prayers can offer comfort and strength when dealing with anxiety and fear. They can help individuals find peace by acknowledging the power of something greater than themselves and seeking guidance and reassurance. Different religious and spiritual traditions offer various prayers and practices to address anxiety and fear.

5. Reframe Challenges as Opportunities for Growth

Every single challenge that you face is an opportunity for growth. Instead of seeing fear as an enemy, start seeing it as a chance to strengthen your faith. Remember the saying, "What doesn't kill you makes you stronger." *James 1:2-4 speaks to this: "Consider it pure joy, my brothers and sisters, whenever you face trials of many kinds, because you know that the testing of your faith produces perseverance."* With each challenge, you're growing stronger, wiser, and more resilient in your faith.

6. Anchor Yourself in God's Promises

The Bible is full of promises from God, and each one is a reminder that He is in control, no matter what we face. Isaiah 41:13 offers us this beautiful assurance: "For I am the Lord your God who takes hold of your right hand and says to you, Do not fear; I will help you." Whenever fear tries to take over, anchor yourself in God's promises. His Word is a firm foundation that fear cannot shake.

7. Surround Yourself with a Supportive Community

You're not meant to battle fear alone. *Ecclesiastes 4:9-10 says, "Two are better than one, because they have a good return for their labor: If either of them falls down, one can help the other up."* Surround yourself with people who encourage you, pray for you, and remind you of God's love and power. Together, you can face fears with a strength that comes from community and faith.

When we rely on God, we discover strength we didn't know we had. (Isaiah 40:31). Fear may try to set in, but with God on our side, it has no chance. He has vowed to stay with us, to support us, and to fight for us. So, the next time fear knocks on your door, remember God is standing with you, he is greater than anything you can imagine. *"The Lord is my strength and my shield; my heart trusts in Him, and He helps me" (Psalm 28:8).* With God, you can overcome any fear.

Safe in the arms of Jesus,
Safe on His gentle breast,
There by His love o'er shaded,
Sweetly my soul shall rest.
Hark! 'tis the voice of angels,
Borne in a song to me,
Over the fields of glory,
Over the jasper sea.

Chorus:
Safe in the arms of Jesus,
Safe on His gentle breast,
There by His love o'er shaded,
Sweetly my soul shall rest.

Safe in the Arms of Jesus

By Fanny J. Crosby

PART 8
LIVING PURPOSEFULLY

"Let your light so shine before men, that they may see your good works, and glorify your Father which is in heaven"
– Matthew 5:16

Have you ever thought about the kind of legacy you'll leave behind? What will people say about you when you're gone? Will your life be something that continues to inspire and impact others, or will it fade into the background, forgotten? Living purposefully means making choices every day that build a life worth celebrating—not just in the short term, but one that leaves a lasting mark, especially in the faith we pass on to others.

Living a life that makes an impact doesn't mean you have to be famous or well-known. It's about living with intention, focusing on how your actions, words, and faith touch the lives of those around you. The Bible says in *Proverbs 13:22, "A good person leaves an inheritance for their children's children."* It's not just about material wealth, it's about leaving behind something more valuable: a legacy of love, faith, and Christ-like living.

Self-Reflection Questions

1. Am I living each day with purpose, or am I merely going through the motions?

2. What kind of legacy do I want to leave for my family, friends, and community?

3. How can I live in a way that reflects Christ and inspires others, even after I'm gone?

Building a Legacy of Faith

The truth is we only have one life. And for believers, that life has a higher purpose: to glorify God and make a difference for His kingdom. We don't know how many days we have on Earth, but the question is, how are we using them? Do we live in a way that draws others to Christ? Will people remember our faith, kindness, or encouragement after we are gone?

James 4:14 reminds us, "You do not know what tomorrow will bring. What is your life? For you are a mist that appears for a little time and then vanishes." This verse is simply saying something – Life is short, and we don't have time to waste. But the good news is, when we live with purpose, we can make every moment count.

Living a Life That Echoes Beyond the Grave

The impact of living a purposeful life extends beyond your lifetime. Your acts can have far-reaching consequences, influencing people's lives long after you die. Consider the persons in your life who have died, but they continue to have an impact on you. Perhaps a grandfather educated you about faith, or a mentor encouraged you during difficult times. Their legacy lives on because they lived purposefully.

Jesus said in *Matthew 5:16, "Let your light shine before others, that they may see your good deeds and glorify your Father in heaven."* That's the kind of life we should aim to live; one where our light continues to shine, guiding others toward God, even after we've left this earth.

Strategy #8: Live a Life Worth Celebrating

1. Invest in Relationships

Your impact will be felt most deeply in the lives of the people around you. Take time to build strong, meaningful relationships. Be a source of encouragement, support, and love to those you meet. In the end, people will remember how you made them feel more than anything else.

2. Share Your Faith Boldly

One of the most lasting legacies you can leave is leading others to Christ. Don't shy away from opportunities to share the hope you have in Him. Whether through your words or your actions, let people see Christ in you.

3. Be Generous with Your Time and Talents

Generosity is not just about money. It's about giving your time, sharing your skills, and helping others where you can. A life spent in service to others is a life that won't be easily forgotten.

4. Live According to God's Will

Align your life with God's plan for you. In *Ephesians 5:15-16, Paul urges us, "Be very careful, then, how you live—not as unwise but as wise, making the most of every opportunity because the days are evil."* When you live in tune with God's will, you are setting yourself up to make a meaningful, eternal impact.

5. Stay Humble and Trust in God's Timing

Proverbs 3:5-6 says, "Trust in the Lord with all your heart and lean not on your own understanding; in all your ways submit to Him, and He will make your paths straight." Living purposefully doesn't mean you'll always know exactly where you're headed, but it means trusting God to lead you in ways that matter, even when it's unclear at the moment.

Living purposefully isn't about making great gestures or becoming noticed by the world. It's about making a difference where it counts the most—where God has placed you. It is about living so that your life leaves a legacy of faith, love, and purpose that will continue to influence people long after you are gone. Let your life be a testimony of God's grace, inspiring generations to come. And as the saying goes, "It's not the years in your life that count, but the life in your years."

By focusing on these principles, you can live a life worth celebrating—one that honors God, touches lives, and leaves a legacy of faith that will never fade away.

"Two little lines I heard one day,
Traveling along life's busy way;
Bringing conviction to my heart,
And from my mind would not depart;
Only one life, 'twill soon be past,
Only what's done for Christ will last."

Only one life, yes only one,
Soon will its fleeting hours be done;
Then, in 'that day' my Lord to meet,
And stand before His Judgment seat;
Only one life, 'twill soon be past,
Only what's done for Christ will last."

Only One Life

By C.T. Studd

PART 9

YOU HAVE POWER OVER DEATH

"O death where is thy sting? O grave, where is thy victory? The sting of death is sin; and the strength of sin is the law. But thanks be to God, which giveth us the victory through our Lord Jesus Christ" – 1 Corinthians 15:55-57

Death can be terribly critical and terrifying. We avoid thinking about or talking about it, and for some, it evokes intense terror. But here's the truth: as a believer, death does not have the final say. You have power over it. It's not just something we hope for; it's a promise from God Himself. Jesus has already defeated death on our behalf, so we no longer have to fear it.

Remember when Jesus said in *John 11:25, "I am the resurrection and the life. The one who believes in me will live, even though they die?"* That wasn't just comforting words for Martha after Lazarus' death—that's a promise for all of us. Jesus didn't just overcome death for Himself, but for every one of us who believes in Him. Death might be the end of our earthly bodies, but it's not the end of us. We have eternal life, and that should radically change how we view death.

Self-Reflection Questions

1. Do I truly believe that death has no power over me?

2. How does my fear of death impact how I live?

3. How can I live more boldly, knowing death has no sting?

Strategy #9: Embracing the Power Over Death

1. Accepting Jesus Christ as Lord and Savior

The first and most crucial step in embracing power over death is to receive Jesus Christ as your Lord and personal Savior. This is the foundation for eternal life and the key to overcoming the fear of death. In Christ, death is not the end—it's a doorway to eternal life with God.

By accepting Jesus, you enter into the fold of believers, where death loses its sting and fear is replaced by the promise of eternal life. As Jesus said in *John 11:25-26, "I am the resurrection and the life. The one who believes in me will live, even though they die, and whoever lives by believing in me will never die."* Coming into Christ transforms your perspective on death from one of fear to one of victory and peace.

This decision is not just about eternity but also about living a life free from the fear of death here and now, knowing that through Christ, death has been conquered. If you haven't yet made this decision, there is no better time than now to welcome Jesus into your heart and embrace the eternal life He promises.

2. Meditate on the Victory of Christ Over Death

When you are now in Christ, you must take your time to get intimate with Jesus and reflect on the ultimate victory that Jesus won on the cross. He didn't just die for our sins; He defeated death entirely. *Revelation 1:18 declares, "I am the Living One; I was dead, and now look, I am alive for ever and ever! And I hold the keys of death and Hades."* That's the Savior we serve—One who holds the keys to death itself. Let that sink in. Meditate on that truth until it becomes part of your mindset.

3. Replace Fear with Faith

When fear of death creeps in, counter it with faith. Speak God's promises over your life. One of the most powerful ways to overcome fear is by holding tightly to His Word. *Hebrews 2:14-15 tells us that "by His death He might break the power of him who holds the power of death—that is, the devil—and free those who all their lives were held in slavery by their fear of death."* Claim that freedom. Every time fear whispers lies, respond with the truth that you've already been set free.

4. Live in the Present Moment with Eternity in Mind

Instead of worrying about when or how death will come, focus on living fully in the moment, with the assurance of eternal life. *James 4:14 reminds us, "You do not know what will happen tomorrow. What is your life? You are a mist that appears for a little while and then vanishes."* This isn't meant to make us feel anxious—it's a reminder to live intentionally, savoring every moment we've been given, knowing eternity awaits.

5. Share the Hope of Eternal Life with Others

If we've found the secret to defeating death—eternal life through Christ—why wouldn't we share that with others? Spreading the message of hope and salvation is one of the most powerful ways to live out our victory over death. *"Go into all the world and preach the gospel to all creation" (Mark 16:15).* When we share the hope we've found in Jesus, it reinforces our own confidence in His power over death.

6. Shift Your Focus from Death to Purpose

Instead of fixating on death, focus on your God-given purpose. You're here for a reason, and death is merely a doorway into a new chapter. *2 Timothy 1:9 reminds us that "He has saved us and called us to a holy life—not because of anything we have done but because of His own purpose and grace."* You have a purpose to fulfill in this life, and fear of death shouldn't distract you from that. Focus on what God has called you to do, and let everything else fade into the background.

7. Trust in God's Perfect Timing

Sometimes, the fear of death comes from not knowing when it will happen. But God's timing is perfect, and our days are in His hands. *Psalm 139:16 says, "All the days ordained for me were written in your book before one of them came to be."* Trust that God knows exactly how long you'll be here, and His timing is never a mistake. Instead of worrying about how much time you have, trust that every day is part of His plan.

8. Celebrate Life Now

Finally, celebrate the life you've been given. Every breath, every moment, is a gift from God. Ecclesiastes 3:12-13 encourages us to enjoy life: "I know that there is nothing better for people than to be happy and to do good while they live. That each of them may eat and drink, and find satisfaction in all their toil—this is the gift of God." When we appreciate the gift of life now, death loses its power over us.

Living in the truth that you have power over death entails accepting the life you've been given and not allowing fear to keep you back. It's about believing that death isn't the end but rather the beginning of something even greater. As you walk in this freedom, recall Jesus' instructions from *John 14:1-3: "Do not let your hearts be troubled."* You believe in God; believe also in me. My father's house contains multiple rooms. I'm heading there to arrange a space for you. So live without the fear of death, knowing that your future is safe in Christ and that death has already been overcome.

Death is nothing at all.

It does not count.

I have only slipped away into the next room.

Nothing has happened.

Everything remains exactly as it was.

I am I, and you are you,

and the old life that we lived so fondly together is untouched, unchanged.

Whatever we were to each other, that we are still.

Call me by the old familiar name.

Speak of me in the easy way which you always used.

Put no difference into your tone.

Wear no forced air of solemnity or sorrow.

Laugh as we always laughed at the little jokes that we enjoyed together.

Play, smile, think of me, pray for me.

Let my name be ever the household word that it always was.

Let it be spoken without effort, without the ghost of a shadow upon it.

Life means all that it ever meant.

It is the same as it ever was.

There is absolute and unbroken continuity.

What is this death but a negligible accident?

Why should I be out of mind because I am out of sight?

I am but waiting for you, for an interval, somewhere very near,
just around the corner.

All is well.

Death is Nothing at All
By Henry Scott Holland

PART 10
(BONUS STRATEGY)

ADDRESSING PAST HURTS
IN RELATIONSHIPS

"Let all bitterness, and wrath, and anger, and clamour, and evil speaking, be put away from you, with all malice: And be ye kind one to another, tenderhearted, forgiving one another, even as God for Christ's sake hath forgiven you"
— Ephesians 4:31-32

Through my experiences, I've come to realize that one of the major causes of fear in relationships is the struggle to forgive and move past a partner's mistakes. This fear, whether it's about trust, past hurts, or emotional wounds, can take a toll not only on the relationship but also on our peace of mind.

When we hold onto unforgiveness while our partner is alive, it can create distance and resentment. But what happens when that partner is no longer around? The regret of not forgiving or healing past wounds can linger far longer than we expect. It can even complicate grief, making it harder to move forward.

This bonus section is dedicated to addressing that fear, showing how we can let go of the past and heal so we can live with fewer regrets and honor our relationships while we still have the chance. After all, forgiveness isn't just for the other person; it's a gift we give ourselves. Just as Christ forgave us, we are called to do the same so we can live freely and fully in our relationships, unburdened by fear or resentment. As *Ephesians 4:32 reminds us, "Be kind and compassionate to one another, forgiving each other, just as in Christ God forgave you."*

Self-Reflection Questions

1. How does my partner's past affect my current relationship?

2. Am I holding on to old fears or insecurities, preventing me from enjoying the present?

3. How can I release my concerns about past mistakes, both in life and in love?

Strategy #10: Let It Go!

No one is perfect, and everyone has a past. But what do you do when your partner's past includes some tough spots? How can you overcome the fear and nervousness that comes with learning about their previous relationships or mistakes? It can be tough.

It's tough to deal with your partner's complex history. Whether it's a messy breakup or a secret from the past, it can be very tough to move on. However, you can do a few things to make it less difficult for you.

1. **First, talk openly and honestly with your partner about their past**

Understanding what happened and why they are keeping any secrets is essential.

- If your partner has a murky past, you may feel uncertain about how to approach the subject. However, having an open and honest talk about your partner's history is critical for developing trust and intimacy in the relationship.

- Prioritize listening over speaking. It can be tempting to offer your own thoughts or experiences, but it is critical to let your spouse to tell their stories at their own speed. Allow them to open up on their own terms.

- Be respectful. Avoid making judgments or criticisms. It is not the time to lecture; instead, focus on understanding your partner's point of view.

- Ask questions. Show that you want to learn more about your partner's past. Allow them to share as much or as little as they feel comfortable with.

- Offer support. Let your lover know you love and support them completely. The conversation will be difficult, so provide reassurance and support along the way.

2. **Give your partner the space and time to process their feelings**

They will come to you when they're ready to talk about it.

- Patience is essential if your partner needs space and time to process their feelings. Allow them the time to come to you on their own terms. In the meantime, you can support them by continuing to be a source of love and reassurance.

- Be understanding. No one is perfect, and everyone has a past. Try to understand your partner's complicated history.

- Trust is a cornerstone of any relationship, but it's hard to trust someone with a murky past. If your partner has been less than forthcoming about their history, giving them the space and time they need to open up is essential.

- Allow details to come to you naturally rather than pressing for them. It's also important to be honest with yourself about your degree of comfort. If your partner's past makes you uncomfortable, it is acceptable to set boundaries.

- Discuss your worries with your spouse and reach an agreement on the level of transparency that is comfortable for both of you. Remember that everyone has a past and deserves the opportunity to go forward.

3. Try to focus on the present and future

It's important to remember that your partner's past does not define them. Give them the chance to move forward without reminding them of their history.

- Focusing on the present and future can be challenging when your partner has a difficult past. However, it's important to remember that your partner's history does not define them. They are capable of change and growth, just like anyone else.

- Focus on the positive aspects of your relationship and your partner's character. For example, spend time together doing things you enjoy. You will build a stronger foundation with your partner when you think positively.

- Talk about your hopes and dreams for the future. Speaking about your ambitions and dreams will make you feel more connected to your partner and remind you of the good things in your relationship.

- Moving on from a partner's complicated background, whether it is a terrible breakup or a hidden past, can be difficult. Use these useful recommendations to help you go forward with your life. When your partner needs aid or reassurance, they will seek it from you.

- When your partner has a challenging past, it might be tough to focus on the present and future. However, you will get over this challenging stage in your relationship with time and patience. Remember that your partner's history does not define them; they are capable of change and growth.

If you want to build a long-lasting, loving relationship, you will need trust, patience, and understanding.

When we come to the end of the road
And the sun has set for me,
I want no rites in a gloom-filled room.
Why cry for a soul set free?

Miss me a little—but not too long,
And not with your head bowed low.
Remember the love that we once shared,
Miss me—but let me go.

For this is a journey we all must take,
And each must go alone.
It's all a part of the Master's plan,
A step on the road to home.

When you are lonely and sick of heart,
Go to the friends we know,
And bury your sorrows in doing good deeds.
Miss me—but let me go.

The End of the Road

By Helen Steiner Rice

A Final Message

At this point, I want to remind you that overcoming the fear of death is not about denying its reality but about embracing the promise of eternal life that God has given us. Death is not the final chapter for those who believe in Christ; it is simply a transition into a more glorious existence. The key to overcoming this fear is to recognize that God has already conquered death through Jesus Christ.

We've walked through practical steps, self-reflection questions, and strategies to help you face your fears, understand your emotions, and lean on God. Fear is natural—it's part of being human—but we do not have to let it control us. As we deepen our faith and reliance on the Creator, we find that fear loses its grip on our lives. *"For God has not given us a spirit of fear, but of power and of love and of a sound mind" (2 Timothy 1:7).*

Reflect on the truth that you were never meant to carry the weight of fear alone. You have a Heavenly Father who walks with you, who comforts you, and who promises that nothing—not even death—can separate you from His love (Romans 8:38-39). Lean into His promises and live boldly, knowing that death is not the end but the beginning of something greater.

Take the strategies you've learned and apply them to your daily life. Talk to God, reflect on His promises, and surround yourself with wise counsel. Don't rush through this process—it's okay to take your time. Healing and peace come in waves, but they are sure to come because God has promised them to you.

When you are faced with life's challenges, remember the words of Jesus like he said in *John 14:27: "Peace I leave with you; my peace I give you. I do not give to you as the world gives. Do not let your hearts be troubled, and do not be afraid."* That peace is yours to claim today and every day moving forward.

You are stronger than you think, and with God's help, you will live a life that is full of purpose, peace, and joy—free from the fear of death. May you find strength, comfort, and courage as you live in the light of God's love and promise of eternal life.

AFTERWORD

We have concluded the strategies for overcoming fear of everything, so it is now time for us to be proactive and plan ahead for our and our families' deaths since we know that we are GONNA DIE, PERIOD!

Don't leave your loved ones wondering what they should do if you were to leave here suddenly. Accidentally or whatever the case may be.

Take care of the Final Expense plans ahead of time. If you don't have Life Insurance, get some and write out your will and estate plan, so when the time comes, family members, and spouses will know what your wishes are.

This will help with the grieving process. They will be afforded the time to grieve and not merely worry about how to pay for your funeral.

Now go, get busy!

APPENDIX

SCRIPTURES FOR OVERCOMING FEAR

These scriptures can provide encouragement and strength when fear threatens to take hold. Meditate on them, memorize them, and repeat them throughout your life as reminders of God's promises.

1. *Isaiah 41:10*

"So do not fear, for I am with you; do not be dismayed, for I am your God. I will strengthen you and help you; I will uphold you with my righteous right hand."

2. *Psalm 27:1*

"The Lord is my light and my salvation—whom shall, I fear? The Lord is the stronghold of my life—of whom shall I be afraid?"

3. *Romans 8:15*

"The Spirit you received does not make you slaves, so that you live in fear again; rather, the Spirit you received brought about your adoption to sonship. And by him we cry, 'Abba, Father.'"

4. *Joshua 1:9*

"Have I not commanded you? Be strong and courageous. Do not be afraid; do not be discouraged, for the Lord your God will be with you wherever you go."

5. *1 John 4:18*

"There is no fear in love. But perfect love drives out fear, because fear has to do with punishment. The one who fears is not made perfect in love."

6. *Psalm 56:3-4*

"When I am afraid, I put my trust in you. In God, whose word I praise—in God I trust and am not afraid. What can mere mortals do to me?"

7. *Philippians 4:6-7*

"Do not be anxious about anything, but in every situation, by prayer and petition, with thanksgiving, present your requests to God. And the peace of God, which transcends all understanding, will guard your hearts and your minds in Christ Jesus."

8. *Matthew 10:28*

"Do not be afraid of those who kill the body but cannot kill the soul. Rather, be afraid of the One who can destroy both soul and body in hell."

9. *Deuteronomy 31:6*

"Be strong and courageous. Do not be afraid or terrified because of them, for the Lord your God goes with you; he will never leave you nor forsake you."

10. *Hebrews 13:6*

"So, we say with confidence, 'The Lord is my helper; I will not be afraid. What can mere mortals do to me?'"

11. *2 Timothy 1:7*

"For the Spirit God gave us does not make us timid, but gives us power, love, and self-discipline."

12. *Psalm 34:4*

"I sought the Lord, and he answered me; he delivered me from all my fears."

13. Isaiah 43:1-2

"But now, this is what the Lord says—he who created you, Jacob, he who formed you, Israel: 'Do not fear, for I have redeemed you; I have summoned you by name; you are mine. When you pass through the waters, I will be with you; and when you pass through the rivers, they will not sweep over you. When you walk through the fire, you will not be burned; the flames will not set you ablaze.'"

14. John 14:27

"Peace, I leave with you; my peace I give you. I do not give to you as the world gives. Do not let your hearts be troubled and do not be afraid."

15. Psalm 23:4

"Even though I walk through the darkest valley, I will fear no evil, for you are with me; your rod and your staff, they comfort me."

16. Romans 8:38-39

"For I am convinced that neither death nor life, neither angels nor demons, neither the present nor the future, nor any powers, neither height nor depth, nor anything else in all creation, will be able to separate us from the love of God that is in Christ Jesus our Lord."

17. Proverbs 3:25-26

"Have no fear of sudden disaster or of the ruin that overtakes the wicked, for the Lord will be at your side and will keep your foot from being snared."

18. Isaiah 54:17

"No weapon forged against you will prevail, and you will refute every tongue that accuses you. This is the heritage of the servants of the Lord, and this is their vindication from me, declares the Lord."

19. 1 Peter 5:7

"Cast all your anxiety on him because he cares for you."

20. Zephaniah 3:17

"The Lord your God is with you, the Mighty Warrior who saves. He will take great delight in you; in his love he will no longer rebuke you, but will rejoice over you with singing."

21. Psalm 118:6

"The Lord is with me; I will not be afraid. What can mere mortals do to me?"

22. Isaiah 12:2

"Surely God is my salvation; I will trust and not be afraid. The Lord, the Lord himself, is my strength and my defense; he has become my salvation."

23. Matthew 6:34

"Therefore, do not worry about tomorrow, for tomorrow will worry about itself. Each day has enough trouble of its own."

24. Luke 12:32

"Do not be afraid, little flock, for your Father has been pleased to give you the kingdom."

25. Revelation 1:17-18

"When I saw him, I fell at his feet as though dead. Then he placed his right hand on me and said: 'Do not be afraid. I am the First and the Last. I am the Living One; I was dead, and now look, I am alive for ever and ever! And I hold the keys of death and Hades.'"

26. John 4:4

"You, dear children, are from God and have overcome them, because the one who is in you is greater than the one who is in the world."

These verses remind us that fear has no place in the life of a believer. God's promises are sure, and His peace is always available. Whenever fear strikes, turn to these words and let them fill you with the courage and confidence that come from knowing that God is in control.

The last verse emphasizes the believer's strength and victory in Christ over the world and its influences.